LIFE IN THE
WOODLANDS

Written by **Rosanne Hooper**

Consultant: Keith Jones
Environmental Consultant

World Book

in association with
WCN

Published in the United States and Canada in 1998 by
World Book, Inc.
525 W. Monroe
20th Floor
Chicago, IL USA 60661
in association with Two-Can Publishing Ltd.

© Two-Can Publishing Ltd, 1998, 1993

Text by Rosanne Hooper
Edited by Lucy Duke
Design by Fionna Robson
U.S. Editor: Karen Ingebretsen, World Book Publishing

**For information on other World Book products,
call 1-800-255-1750, x 2238, or visit us at our website at
www.worldbook.com**

ISBN: 0-7166-5215-3 (hard cover)
ISBN: 0-7166-5216-1 (soft cover)
LC: 97-62318

1 2 3 4 5 6 7 8 9 10 01 00 99 98 (hc)
1 2 3 4 5 6 7 8 9 10 01 00 99 98 (sc)

Printed in Hong Kong

Photographic Credits
pp 4-5 Planet Earth/John Lythgoe p6 Bruce Coleman/Robert P Carr p7 (top) Zefa/T Martin p7 (bottom) Zefa/Robert Jureit p8 (top) Zefa p8 (bottom) Frank Lane/M J Thomas p9 (top) Bruce Coleman/Jane Burton p9 (bottom) Zefa p10 Planet Earth/Ken King p11 (right) Zefa/G Scott p12 Bruce Coleman/Scott Nielson p13 Bruce Coleman/Hans Reinhard p14 Zefa/P & T Leeson p15 (top) Planet Earth/William M Smithey Jr p15 (bottom) Bruce Coleman/Joseph Van Wormer p16 Zefa/E & P Bauer p17 (top) Bryan & Cherry Alexander p17 (bottom) Biofotos/Heather Angel p18 Frank Lane/E & D Hasking p19 (right) Image Bank/Grant Faint p19 (left) Zefa pp 20-21 Bruce Coleman/Colin Molyneux p22 Still/Mark Edwards p23 Panos/Penny Tweedie

Front cover: Images Colour Library. Back cover: Bruce Coleman

Illustrations by Madeleine David. Story illustrations by Ruth Rivers.

CONTENTS

Looking at Woodlands 4

Where in the World? 6

Seasonal Cycles 8

Leaf Life 10

Forest Birds 12

Forest Vegetarians 14

Forest Hunters 16

Woodland Resources 18

Shrinking Woodlands 20

Saving Our Woodlands 22

Bombo Meets Mother Eagle 24

True or False? 29

Glossary 30

Index 32

All words marked in **bold** can be found in the glossary.

LOOKING AT WOODLANDS

Woodlands are rich in animal and plant life. It is mainly the trees that keep the forest alive by providing food and **habitats** for wildlife.

There are many kinds of woodland, which are usually named after the types of trees that grow there. **Deciduous forests** have broadleaved trees such as oak, maple, and beech. They lose their leaves in winter and change color with the seasons.

Coniferous forests have **evergreen** trees such as pines and firs. These trees have needle-shaped leaves, which stay on the branches all year around. **Mixed woodlands** contain both coniferous and deciduous trees.

Temperate **rain forests** are warm and damp, but less so than tropical rain forests. They are very rich in unusual **species**, including the giant redwood trees of North America.

A TREE'S LIFE STORY

We can tell the age of a tree by the number of growth rings it has. Most trees grow a new layer of wood each year. Each layer makes another ring, which we can see when a tree is cut through. Some ancient bristlecone pines in North America have nearly 5,000 rings. The rings record hot, cold, and wet weather; pollution; and disease. Scientists can use them to learn about the climate and conditions of ancient times.

WHERE IN THE WORLD?

Because most land is found in the northern half of the world, most woodlands and forests are found here too. They lie between the cold Arctic and the hot, humid tropics. A band of coniferous forests runs across the north from Alaska to Siberia. Deciduous forests grow throughout North America, Europe, and Asia. Mixed woodlands grow in some of these areas, too. There are pockets of temperate rain forest in The United States, China, Japan, and New Zealand. Tropical rain forests grow near the Equator.

▶ In deciduous forests, the leaves on the trees lose their green color, dry out, and fall in autumn.

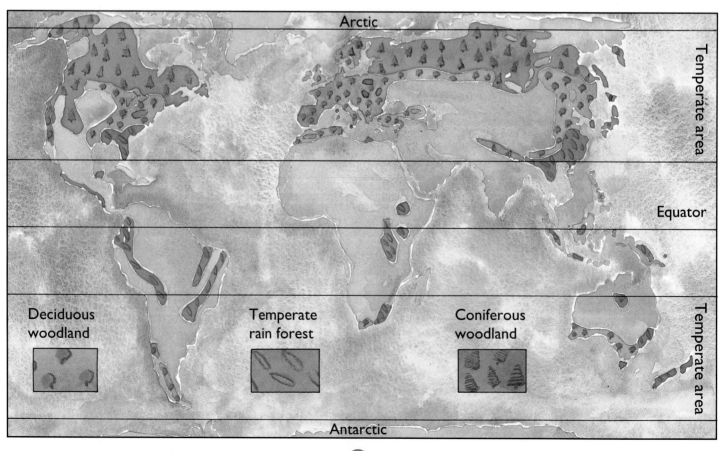

Arctic

Temperate area

Equator

Deciduous woodland

Temperate rain forest

Coniferous woodland

Temperate area

Antarctic

▲ The mountains in Colorado have mixed woodlands. Deciduous trees show their bright autumn colors, while snow covers the coniferous trees.

◄ Temperate rain forests have some of the world's tallest trees. Black bears, black-tailed deer, and the tiniest moles also live there.

Until a few hundred years ago, most of Europe and North America was covered with forest. People say that a squirrel could have crossed a whole **continent** without touching the ground. Today, only a fraction of that woodland is left. Much disappeared to make way for farming and building. The original **wildwoods** are now rare, although areas do still exist, for example in Poland, France, Great Britain, and North America.

SEASONAL CYCLES

Life in a woodland is always changing. In early spring, the days grow longer and warmer. **Migrating** birds arrive and build their nests. Flowers appear on the woodland floor. The first of the baby animals are born. They feed on the new green leaves so that they can grow strong before the cold weather comes. Sometimes animals have a second family to make sure that some young survive. When the summer comes, the forest buzzes with activity. Insects hatch, and woodland creatures feast on the nuts and fruits growing around them.

▲ The forest floor sometimes looks bare, because leaves and branches block out the light. Few plants can survive in the dark, shady area below.

◄ Most woodland flowers, such as these bluebells and red campions, bloom in late spring and early summer. They have to make the most of the sunlight to help them grow before the leaves on the trees open fully and cast a shadow over them. The range of species of flowers growing in an area of woodland can tell us about its age. Older woodlands often have a much wider variety than younger ones, and there are some species that can be found only in ancient woodlands.

◀ Woodland creatures such as hedgehogs, dormice, and woodchucks hibernate through the winter. They curl up into a tight ball and stay fast asleep. Their bodies cool down to save energy. Squirrels, bears, and badgers doze during the cold months, waking and moving around from time to time. Squirrels nibble nuts they stored in the autumn.

▼ The coats of some deer species change color with the seasons. This helps them to hide from **predators** when the landscape around them changes. An ermine's coat also changes, from brown in the summer to white in the winter.

Gradually the days grow shorter and colder. Trees prepare for the winter, changing color and then shedding their leaves. Animals grow thick coats and gather food that must last until spring. Some animals **hibernate** to escape the cold. Many species of birds migrate to warmer lands. Snow covers young plants like a blanket to protect them from frost. In the spring, the cycle begins again.

LEAF LIFE

Trees are a source of life for all the plants and animals in a woodland. They are **ecosystems** in themselves. The oak tree alone offers food and shelter to more than 300 species of insects. Most woodland trees grow from nuts that are spread by animals or, like other woodland plants, from seeds carried by the wind. This is why woodland flowers such as forget-me-nots are so small and hidden. They do not need to attract insects or birds to help them reproduce.

▶ American leaf-cutter ants take pieces of leaves into their nests. They use the leaves to fertilize the tiny fungus on which they feed.

LIFE IN A LOG

Nothing is wasted in a woodland. A fallen log lying on the forest floor gives food to other living things and is soon humming with new life. First the slugs and woodlice arrive. They are eaten by centipedes and spiders. A year or so later, fungi, mosses, and flowers coat the bark. Beetles chew into the wood, and reptiles such as lizards and snakes lie in wait for them. By the following year, hundreds of insects are busy laying eggs and storing food. Birds come to feed on them. Finally, the insects help the log to crumble, and it becomes part of the soil and helps new trees and other plants to grow.

Each species of tree grows best in a particular kind of soil and climate. Ancient oaks are at home in western Europe, as are beeches. These also grow in North America, along with giant redwoods and maples. In Russia and Canada, pines, larches, and other coniferous trees make up the biggest forests in the world. Massive kauri trees are native to New Zealand, where Maori people once made war canoes from them.

▲ The needles on a pine tree help it during the winter. When the ground is frozen, water cannot reach the trunk through the roots. Instead, the needles have a coating of wax that keeps the water inside them from escaping. The shape of the needles makes it difficult for snow to settle on the branches. Their dark color also helps them to absorb extra warmth from the sun.

▲ Many forest trees produce fruits and berries. These make a good meal for insects and birds such as the cedar waxwing of North America. People also eat some woodland fruits and can make use of every part of a tree, even the bark. Oak bark is sometimes used as a medicine for sore throats and nosebleeds, while witch hazel bark and leaves can soothe cuts and bruises.

FOREST BIRDS

Each woodland bird has its favorite niche or place in the forest. Eagles and hawks keep a lookout high in the branches. Owls and nuthatches peer out of old tree holes, and capercaillie rummage about on the forest floor. In spring, the forest hums with birdsongs from dawn to dusk. This is how birds claim their **territory** and attract a mate. Some give their mates a special **courtship display**. Waxwings give each other "presents," while male scarlet tanagers have bright, eye-catching red feathers.

Adult birds are always busy. They need to feed their chicks every few hours. Some have adapted especially to forest foods. Crossbills hook pine nuts out of cones with their unusual crossed-over beaks. Nutcrackers wedge nuts in crevices and drill out the kernel. They store nuts for the winter but sometimes forget where they left them. Woodpeckers eat ants in summer and pine nuts in winter. Nuthatches can hang upside down on tree trunks to catch insects. Sapsuckers trap insects in tree sap.

WINTER HOLIDAYS

Some birds migrate to escape the cold winter. Warblers steer by the stars to find their way, while thrushes follow the sun. Young cuckoos fly all the way to Africa without their parents. They all fly back again the following spring to build their nests.

◀ Woodpeckers use their beaks as high-speed drills to make holes in trees for nesting or hunting for food. They have very long, sticky tongues that they keep curled up inside their heads. When they have made a hole in the bark or wood of a tree, they reach their tongues inside and pick up insects.

▼ Tawny owls feed on mice and voles, which they catch from the forest floor and surrounding countryside. But they are under threat. Their woodland habitat has been destroyed in many places, forcing them to hunt in towns and near busy roads.

FOREST VEGETARIANS

Trees provide a larder for thousands of forest creatures. Insect **larvae** burrow into wood. Caterpillars chew leaf edges. Plant bugs suck tree sap. Deer, moose, rabbits, and hares munch new green shoots. In winter they eat nuts, berries, and bark, as do squirrels and wild boar. Worms and mites working deep in the forest floor transform dead leaves, which fall in the autumn, into new soil for the following spring.

▶ Beavers are expert engineers. They cut down whole trees with their sharp teeth to build dams and lodges in which to live. These homes have an underwater entrance to keep predators from getting in. Each part of the dam and lodge is built so that there will be no flooding.

FIGHTING FACTS

● Male deer fight "duels" in the breeding season. They use their antlers as weapons. The strongest one wins a whole herd of female deer with which to mate.

● When in danger, a squirrel can stay quite still for half an hour. It warns its family by thumping its feet and slapping its tail on the ground. If it is in a tree when an enemy is near, it drops down to a safe lower branch.

► Moose feed on leaves, tree shoots, twigs, and grasses. They have very soft, pliable lips and long muzzles that they use to delicately pick juicy leaves from high branches. They often bend young trees by pushing against the trunks as they reach up for the tender leaves growing at the top. They also eat plants from the bottom of forest lakes and prefer to live in swampy woodland areas.

▼ Chipmunks belong to the same family as squirrels. They burrow underground and build their nests in tunnels. Here they store food such as seeds and nuts that will last through their winter hibernation.

Many plant-eating woodland insects are very secretive in order to avoid predators. The female sawfly hides her eggs in pine needles. She slices the needles open with special "saws" on her legs and lays her eggs inside. Weevils roll up leaves into tubes and hide their eggs inside. Other insects disguise themselves to look like buds, bird droppings, twigs, or dead leaves to fool their enemies.

FOREST HUNTERS

Big forest **carnivores** are becoming rare. There are more of them in the coniferous forests of the north, because they are farther from the people who affect their woodland environment. Bears and wolves have suffered badly from the loss of large areas of forest, which have been cleared to make room for new buildings or farmland.

Lynx and wildcats sit high in the trees ready to pounce on small **rodents**. Wolves hunt together in packs for caribou, moose, and deer. They waste nothing and may bury leftovers for another day.

▼ Like badgers, wolves, and bats, foxes usually wait until dark to venture out of their dens to hunt. When cubs are a few weeks old, their mother takes them out for hunting lessons.

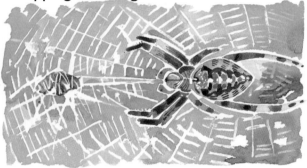

▲ Northern European forest dwellers such as the Lapp people herd reindeer as part of their traditional way of life. But now some of the forests where they spend the winter are threatened by logging companies.

◄ Bears love to eat fish. They wait in streams for salmon to leap out of the water. They also climb trees to raid insect nests in search of honey.

There were once many groups of **nomadic** forest people, such as **Native** Americans who hunted moose, deer, and beaver. A few still live as their ancestors did, but many were driven out by European settlers. The forests where they used to live are now being destroyed by developers who plan to exploit their **resources**.

WOODLAND RESOURCES

We all depend on the forest. In the north of the world, we use wood to make our lives comfortable. Many things that we use every day, from tables and chairs to pianos and guitars, begin as a tree. We turn wood into paper, then into books, newspapers, and packaging. Some of us use as many as 100 sheets of paper in a day. In the south of the world, wood is essential to survival. Half of all the trees cut down are used for fuel.

All sorts of fruits, nuts, seeds, and spices come from the world's forests. Chestnuts and hazelnuts grow in deciduous woodlands. Apple, apricot, peach, and plum trees are traditional woodland species. Today, they are cultivated, and the fruits are sold fresh or dry. The sap from maple trees makes maple syrup.

However, even with all these products, we take very little food from the forest compared to the quantity of wood we use.

▼ This Gambian woman carries home a supply of wood, which she will burn to provide heat, cook food, and heat water.

CORK FACTS

Cork comes from the bark of the cork oak tree. It is stripped off only once every 10 years to allow the tree to grow a new layer. When the bark is dry it is processed to make floor tiles and corks for bottles.

▲ Paper comes from coniferous trees like the spruce, pine, and larch. Millions of these trees are cut down every year. The wood is chopped up, pulped, mixed with water, and spread out to dry. It is then used to make newsprint, books, packaging, and other paper products.

▲ The simple pine tree gives us pine nuts, paper, glue, and perfumes.

In addition to being an important resource for people, woodlands house millions of unique plants and animals. They also hold soil in place so it does not wash away. They provide moisture for rain, and they help to keep our climate in balance.

SHRINKING WOODLANDS

It is not just tropical rain forests that are disappearing today. Ancient woodlands are going too. In Canada, two-thirds of the forests have already vanished. In North America, only 1 tree in every 20 is spared.

Half of Britain's wildwoods have disappeared in the last century. Beavers, bears, and lynx went with them. In Scandinavia, many of the

newly planted forests contain only one tree species.

Trees are cut down to make way for homes, farming, and industry. Some are destroyed by forest fires, others by storms. "Acid rain" caused by factory fumes kills trees and pollutes the soil, rivers, and lakes. Germany's white fir trees have been damaged in this way. Hunting, too, endangers animals. For example, there are very few bison left living wild in the world today.

The results are serious. Rare plants and animals are losing their habitats. Soil is **eroding**, climate patterns are changing, and droughts and floods are increasing as the world gradually heats up. We need to act now. Our future depends on it.

DID YOU KNOW?

● When logging companies cut down trees in North America, a quarter of them are not used and are left on the ground to rot.

● Since 1950, over half the world's trees have disappeared, and many species are now under threat.

● We are losing 68 species of wildlife every day. By the year 2000, one in every six will be gone. Not since the time of the dinosaurs have so many unique species disappeared every day.

SAVING OUR WOODLANDS

All over the world, people are working to protect woodlands and their wildlife. Environmental groups are campaigning to save endangered species. The sable used to be killed for its hair, which was used to make paintbrushes. Happily, it has been saved from **extinction**. National Parks in many places allow animals to live and breed in peace. People are not allowed to hunt or light fires in these areas.

We need to take even better care of our woodlands. In Sweden and Finland, more trees are planted than cut down. But only one or two species are planted, so the wildlife is suffering. It needs a variety of trees to make up its true habitat. If we doubled the amount of paper we recycle, we could reduce by half the number of trees we cut down. This would help to preserve the rich, ancient forests that remain. Governments need to take urgent action to reduce pollution and prevent further **deforestation** and loss of species. They could also encourage **conservation**.

▲ Some Hindus in parts of India hold special ceremonies in which they offer gifts to trees to show their respect for nature and living things.

◀ Tree-planting programs are being set up in every country. These children in Sri Lanka are taking seedlings to a tree nursery to plant.

The Chipko Movement was started by a group of Indian women who saved their forest from loggers by hugging the trees. When the axemen came, the women surrounded the trunks and refused to move. They explained how the trees prevent the soil from eroding and help to keep the rivers flowing. The government agreed to stop the logging.

WHAT YOU CAN DO

● Join a conservation group. Support its work, find out more, and even help to protect a rare bird or animal.

● Collect a few acorns and conkers in the autumn. Plant them in your yard, at school, or in a patch of wasteland. Take care of them and watch them grow.

● Start a paper-recycling or tree-planting program at school or where you live.

● Encourage your family to buy environment-friendly and recycled products.

BOMBO MEETS MOTHER EAGLE

For thousands of years people have told stories about the world around them. Often these stories try to explain something that people do not understand. This tale is told by the Iroquois people of the forests of the Eastern United States.

Bombo was a great hunter. He lived deep in the forests of Pennsylvania and caught more deer than any hunter his people had ever known. Every morning he set out with his special green bow and his long, sharp arrows. Every lunchtime he returned with a deer slung over his shoulder.

Bombo had magic power. All he had to do was call to the deer, and they would come and graze near his home. But he was not satisfied. He wanted more.

One day he decided to test his power. He called to the eagles, "Hey, Eagles, I have fresh meat here for you. Come and take it to your aeries." Golden eagles swooped down from all directions. There were males, females, and even some young ones who had only just learned to fly. But as they reached the feast, Bombo shot them one by one and stole their feathers.

The next day, Bombo called the eagles again. Eighteen female birds glided majestically down to find food for their chicks. He aimed his arrow and was just about to shoot when a voice behind him said, "Stop!" Bombo swung around in surprise. Standing before him was his best friend, Lilo.

"This is very dangerous, Bombo," he warned. "You must stop immediately. The animals are upset and angry. It is wrong to shoot the eagles and take their feathers."

"Nonsense," replied Bombo. "I'm not doing any harm. Look at my beautiful feather collection. I can make some amazing arrows now."

"You're wrong," said Lilo. "I'm your friend, and I don't want to see you hurt, but if you don't stop, the animals will teach you a lesson."

But Bombo ignored his friend and walked off, shaking his head.

The next day Bombo called the eagles for the third time. To his surprise, nothing happened. The forest remained silent and still. As Bombo strained his ears for some sound from the eagles, he thought that he could hear a faint humming. Suddenly, a gigantic dark shape loomed out of the sky toward him. It was the mother of all eagles – and she was very, very angry. Bombo had never been so terrified in his life. He took one look at her and ran off as fast as he could. He spotted a hollow log and quickly wriggled inside, but Mother Eagle was just behind him. She grabbed him with her huge claws and swept him up into the air with two angry beats of her powerful wings.

They flew up and up until the forest looked like a green carpet below them. Bombo's heart was beating faster and faster. He felt dizzy. The forest seemed to turn from green to blue. Mother Eagle swooped up and down and around in circles until Bombo thought he would die. As they soared up again, he thought he glimpsed the edge of the forest way below. He panicked. Were they about to leave his home altogether?

All of a sudden, they were heading straight for a huge tree. Just as Bombo was sure they were going to crash, Mother Eagle swooped down into her aerie, dropped him into her nest with her chicks, and flew off.

Bombo was terrified. How would he get home now? Suddenly he had an idea. In his pocket he had some dried meat and leather thongs. He offered the meat to the eaglets, who gobbled it up greedily, then he tied their beaks with the thongs.

When Mother Eagle came back with food for her chicks and saw what Bombo had done, she was furious.

"This is wrong, Bombo. Untie them this minute," she cried.

"No," replied Bombo. "I won't untie them until you promise to let me go."

For two days Mother Eagle tried to unpick the tight leather thongs with her sharp beak, but to no avail. Meanwhile, her chicks grew thinner and thinner. They were soon so weak that they could hardly stand up. Mother Eagle flew off around the forest with a grave look on her face.

Finally, she returned to the nest.

"I'll make a pact with you, Bombo," she said. "If you promise never to kill another eagle without permission from the Spirit World, and if you untie my chicks this minute, you may safely go back to your home."

"I promise," he replied, untying the thongs so that the hungry chicks could eat at last. As Mother Eagle fed her family, Bombo saw them grow big and strong right before his eyes. Suddenly, before he could even blink, he found himself back, safe and sound, in his own home.

From that day on, whenever Bombo caught a deer, he called the eagles and invited them to come and share the meal in safety. He never killed another eagle, and the only feathers he collected were the ones the eagles left for him. From then on, all the hunters in the forest followed Bombo's example. The eagles and the forest people understood one another at last.

TRUE OR FALSE?

Which of these facts are true and which ones are false?
If you have read this book carefully, you will know the answers.

1. Most woodlands are in the top half of the world.

2. Beavers warn their families of trouble by thumping their feet and slapping their tails.

3. Ermines have a white coat in summer and a brown coat in winter.

4. Nuthatches stand upside down on tree trunks to catch insects.

5. A woodpecker has such a long tongue that it has to keep it curled up inside its head.

6. Waxwings have bright red feathers to attract a mate.

7. If a wolf is attacked, its tail can drop off to allow it to escape.

8. Indian women saved their forest by hugging the trees.

9. Rabbits have special skin flaps so that they can fly through the forest.

10. Maori people used pine trees to make war canoes.

GLOSSARY

● **Carnivore** An animal that eats other animals to survive. An herbivore only eats plants. An omnivore eats both meat and plants.

● **Coniferous forest** A forest made up of evergreen trees, which have cones and needles.

● **Conservation** The protection and preservation of wildlife and the environment in which it lives.

● **Courtship display** When a bird, animal, or insect performs or changes color to attract a mate.

● **Continent** One of the world's large land masses, usually divided into a number of countries.

● **Deciduous forest** A forest made up of trees that lose their leaves in winter.

● **Deforestation** Destroying large areas of woodland to make room for building, mining, or farming.

● **Ecosystem** A community of plants and animals and its environment.

● **Eroding** The wearing away of soil or land by wind or water. Trees help to prevent erosion.

● **Evergreens** Trees and plants that have green leaves all year around.

● **Extinction** When a species dies out completely, it is said to be extinct.

● **Habitat** The natural environment of a plant or animal.

● **Hibernate** To sleep during the winter. While hibernating, animals use very little energy, and many do not need food.

● **Larvae** The young of some insect species before they develop and grow wings.

● **Migrate** To travel long distances every year. Many birds migrate from their summer breeding grounds to warmer winter feeding places.

● **Mixed woodlands** Forests with evergreen trees as well as seasonal deciduous trees.

● **Native** A plant, animal, or person whose family originally comes from the area in which it lives.

● **Nomadic** People who move from place to place in search of pasture and food are nomadic.

● **Predator** An animal that hunts and kills other creatures.

● **Rain forest** A thick, evergreen forest with high levels of rainfall. Temperate rain forests are warm and moist with most rainfall in winter. Tropical rain forests are hot and wet with heavy rainfall all year around.

● **Resources** Natural materials, such as wood, taken from their environment and used by people.

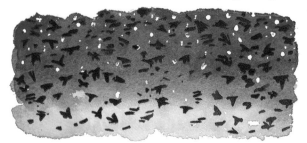

● **Rodent** A small mammal, such as a squirrel or beaver, with strong front teeth that it uses for gnawing hard objects.

● **Species** A group of animals or plants that shares the same characteristics and can breed with one another.

● **Territory** The area where an animal lives and breeds.

● **Woodland** An area of land in temperate countries, where many trees grow close together.

● **Wildwoods** Ancient woodlands in their natural state, inhabited by their original species.

INDEX

bears 7, 9, 16, 20
beavers 14, 17, 20,
birds 8, 11, 12-13

Chipko Movement 23
chipmunks 15
coniferous forests 4, 6, 16, 19
cork 19

deciduous forests 4, 6, 7, 18
deer 7, 9, 14, 16, 17
deforestation 13, 17, 20-21
dormice 9, 16

ermines 9
erosion 21, 23

flowers 8, 10
forest floor 8, 10, 13, 14
foxes 16
fruits 8, 11, 18

hibernation 9, 15

insects 8, 10, 11, 12, 14, 15

kauri trees 11

Lapp people 17
leaves 6, 8, 9, 10, 15
logging 21, 23

Maori people 11
maple trees 4, 11, 18
migration 8, 9, 12
mixed woodlands 4, 7
moose 14, 15, 16, 17

nuts 8, 10, 12, 14, 18

oak trees 4, 10, 11, 19
owls 12, 13

paper 18, 19, 22, 23
pine trees 5, 11, 19
plants 8, 9, 10, 15, 19, 21
pollution 5, 21, 22

rain forests
    temperate 4, 6, 7
    tropical 4, 20
redwood trees 4, 11

seeds 10, 15, 18
shrews 16
soil 10, 11, 19, 21, 23
spiders 10, 16
squirrels 7, 9, 14, 15

tree rings 5
tree worship 23

wildwoods 7, 20-21
wood, uses of 18, 19
woodpeckers 12